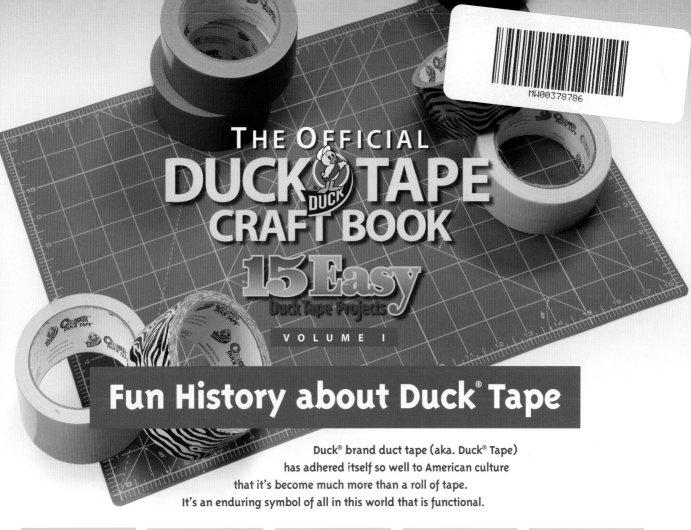

THE OFFICIAL DUCK TAPE CRAFT BOOK

15 Easy Duck Tape Projects

VOLUME I

Fun History about Duck® Tape

Duck® brand duct tape (aka. Duck® Tape)
has adhered itself so well to American culture
that it's become much more than a roll of tape.
It's an enduring symbol of all in this world that is functional.

1939

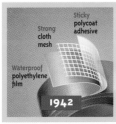
1942

1946

1976

Today

So how did this sticky wonder come about? It was World War II and there was a need for a strong, flexible, durable, waterproof tape that could seal canisters, repair cracked windows, repair trucks and help the war effort in general. Permacell, a division of the Johnson and Johnson Company, stepped up to this challenge.

Using medical tape as a base, they applied two new technologies. Polycoat adhesives gave the tape its unshakable stick and polyethylene coating allowed them to laminate the tape to a cloth backing, making it extremely strong and flexible. The resulting tape was nicknamed "Duck Tape" for its ability to repel water, while ripping easily into strips for fast convenient use.

After the war the tape was put to the more civilian use of holding ducts together. So the product changed from a nameless army green tape to the familiar gray duct tape.

Thirty years later, Jack Kahl, former CEO of Manco, Inc., changed the name of the product to Duck® Tape and put 'Manco T. Duck' on the Duck® Tape logo, giving personality to a commodity product. Manco, Inc. also began to shrink-wrap and label the product, making it easier to stack for retailers, and easier to distinguish different grades for customers.

Now, over 50 years after its invention, Duck® Tape is sold in more than 25 colors, prints, and college logos and is touted by its followers for having a nearly endless amount of uses. What will happen to Duck® Tape next?

Suggested supplies for Duck® Tape crafts

Supplies:

Variety of colors and prints of Duck® Brand Duct Tape.

Scissors recommended: Westcott® Non-Stick Titanium scissors

Craft board

Ruler

Single hole punch

Pen

Stickers for decoration

Available Colors and Patterns for sale:

Aqua

Beige

Black

Blue

Brown

Butterflies

Checker

Chrome

Cosmic Tie Dye

Digital Camo

Dragons

Electric Blue

Flames

Green

Gold

Houndstooth

Maroon

Neon Green

Neon Orange

Neon Pink

Paint Splatter

Pink Zebra

Polkadot Blue

Polkadot Multicolor

Polkadot Pink

Purple

Red

Spotted Leopard™

Skulls

Totally Tie-Dye

White

Yellow

Zig-Zag Zebra®

Belt 4
Bookcover 5
Bookmark 6
Cell Phone Case 6
Coin Bank 7
Daisy/Daisy Pen 8
Drink Koozie 9
Flip Flops 10
Hair Bow 10
Luggage Tab 11
Picture Frame 12
Purse 13
Rose 14
Wallet 15
Wristlet 16

Duck® Tape has been known to fix everything around the house. Now with the help of this book, we invite you to explore your creative side using Duck® Tape as a craft medium.

Using the basic skills learned from the crafts in this book, we hope to help you build a fundamental base to expand your creativity using Color Duck® Tape.

Stick out from the crowd with our new Duck® Tape crafts. Getting bored with that design? Create a new one! It's up to you and the sky is the limit.

Remember it is 1% inspiration. 99% Duck® Tape.™

 Trust E. Tips: Look for the Trust E. Duck symbol for helpful Ducktivity Tips that will make your Duck® Tape projects really stick out!

Duck® Tape Fabric

Supplies

Duck® Brand Duct Tape

Scissors

Ruler or measuring tape

❶ Start your Duck® Tape fabric by cutting a strip of Duck® Tape to the desired length and lay it sticky side up on your work surface.

❷ Cut another strip of Duck® Tape the same length.

❸ Place the second strip sticky side up so it slightly overlaps the edge of the first strip.

❹ Cut and overlap the tape strips until you have the appropriate width and length for your fabric project.

❺ Cut a strip to lay across the strips that are sticky side up. Place the strips vertically sticky side down. Remember to overlap edges.
Note: These strips should be placed vertically sticky side down.

❻ Continue to lay strips vertically, sticky side down, until all of the sticky sides of the "bottom" strips are covered. Remember to slightly overlap edges.

❼ Trim off sticky edges.

Belt

1 Measure your waist with a measuring tape or string. Cut two pieces of Duck® Tape according to your waist measurements. Cut the tape a couple inches longer than your waist measurements to ensure it will be long enough to loop through the belt buckle.

2 Take both pieces of tape and stick them together, sticky side to sticky side. Make sure to leave about ¼ inch of the bottom piece of tape exposed with the sticky side up. Once both pieces are stuck together, fold the exposed bottom piece of tape over the top side creating a seal.

3 Trim off the ends of the belt for a clean look.

4 Enjoy decorating it with your favorite color Duck® Tape. Try creating stripes, polka dots, or any other fun design.

Belt Buckle

5 Cut a 2 inch section of Duck® Tape and cut out a "T" shape. Fold the bottom of the "T" up to stick to the top of the shape. It should look like a cross. Place the tape on the belt and wrap it around the buckle to secure it in place.

6 Repeat Step 5 to make another "T" shape.

7 Cut another piece of tape and wrap it horizontally around the base of the buckle.

8 Cut the opposite end of the belt into a point.

9 Take your hole punch or grommet punch and punch holes through the tape making sure to space them to create a belt that will be appropriately sized.

10 Cut a 4 inch piece of tape and fold it in half. Fold it around the belt and tape the ends to the bottom to create the belt loop.

Be sure to leave enough space for the belt to slide through.

Supplies

Duck® Brand Duct Tape

Belt Buckle

Scissors

Craft Board

Measuring Tape/ String

Hole Punch/ Grommet Punch

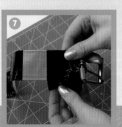

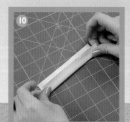

Bookcover

For writing on Duck® Tape, we recommend Sharpie® Paint Markers.

For personalizing your book cover with names, shapes, or letters try our easy to use Duck® Tape Sheets on grid liner!

Supplies

Duck® Brand Duct Tape

Textbook

Invisible tape

Brown paper grocery bag

Scissors

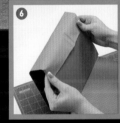

❶ Cut open a brown paper bag along one seam (from top to bottom) and then cut off the bottom (base) of the bag. Lay it out flat on your work surface. **Note:** If the paper bag is printed on one side, lay the printed side facing you.

❷ Place the book in the middle of the bag to measure.

❸ Fold the paper up along the top and bottom of the book..

❹ Fold the side of the bag over the front cover of the book.

❺ Repeat step 4 with the other side of the book. **Note:** If you need to, use small pieces of invisible tape to make the paper bag cover stay in place.

❻ Place the book cover over the book ends to secure it in place.

❼ Cover the paper bag book cover with your favorite color(s) of Duck® Tape. **Note:** Removing the paper bag and laying it flat on your work surface may make it easier to cover it with Duck® Tape.

❽ Be sure to cut the strips of Duck® Tape long enough to cover the book from side to side or top to bottom, depending on which direction you choose.

❾ The tape should be long enough to wrap around the inside of the book to cover the paper bag flaps, making the cover look seamless.

❿ Be careful not to tape to the inside of the book, as this may cause damage when the cover is removed at the end of the school year.

⓫ Get creative! Use multiple colors to create unique patterns or add your favorite embellishments. It's easy to write on Duck® Tape, too!

Bookmark

Supplies

Duck® Brand Duct Tape

Scissors

Ruler or measuring tape

Single hole punch (optional)

Yarn or ribbon (optional)

1 Choose your favorite color of Duck® Tape and cut two strips each measuring 5 inches in length and make a piece of Duck® Tape fabric out of it.

Note: Refer to page 3 for instructions.

2 Trim off sticky edges and round the corner of the bookmark if so desired.

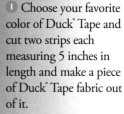

3 Use a hole punch to make a hole at the top of the bookmark. Be careful not to make it too close to the top edge.

4 Loop yarn or ribbon through the hole to make a decoration for the top of the bookmark.

5 Decorate your bookmark with your favorite Duck® Tape colors and designs!

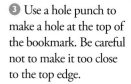

Cell Phone Case

1 Take the string and wrap it around your phone to measure the width. Then measure the length and height with a ruler.

2 Create a piece of Duck® Tape fabric to fit your cell phone's measurements, making sure to trim the ragged edges to ensure clean lines.

3 Cut off a 1½ inch strip of Duck® Tape to use as a placeholder. Wrap the sheet around the phone and stick the 1½ inch strip of Duck® Tape on the seams.

4 Cut a strip of Duck® Tape long enough to cover the place holder piece and seams of the cell phone case.

5 Cut a 3 inch piece of tape and lay it sticky side up. Then place a 1 inch piece of tape in the center of the longer piece.

6 Tape the Duck® Tape strip to the bottom of the case making sure the 1 inch piece on top covers the opening of the bottom of the case. This will protect your phone from sticking to the tape.

7 Place another piece of Duck® Tape to the back of the case, where the seam is, to create a smooth line.

For a seamless cell phone case try using a Duck® Tape Sheet. Each sheet is 8 ¼" x 10" in size.

Supplies

- Duck® Brand Duct Tape
- Tissue Box
- Scissors
- Craft Board (Optional)

1 Cut strips of Duck® Tape to fit your tissue box. **Note:** Cover the corners of the box first to ensure clean smooth lines on your coin bank.

2 Cover your tissue box with the Duck® Tape strips you cut in step 1. Make sure to leave the tissue opening on top uncovered so you can put your money in it. Use different colors of Duck® Tape to create a unique look.

3 To open, cut a small slit in the bottom of the tissue box to access your money. Once empty, simply seal the hole with another strip of Duck® Tape and start saving for your next roll of fun!

Decorate your coin box with different designs, jewels, or any creative aspect to make it one of a kind!

Supplies

- Duck® Brand Duct Tape
- Cell phone (For measurement)
- String
- Ruler
- Scissors

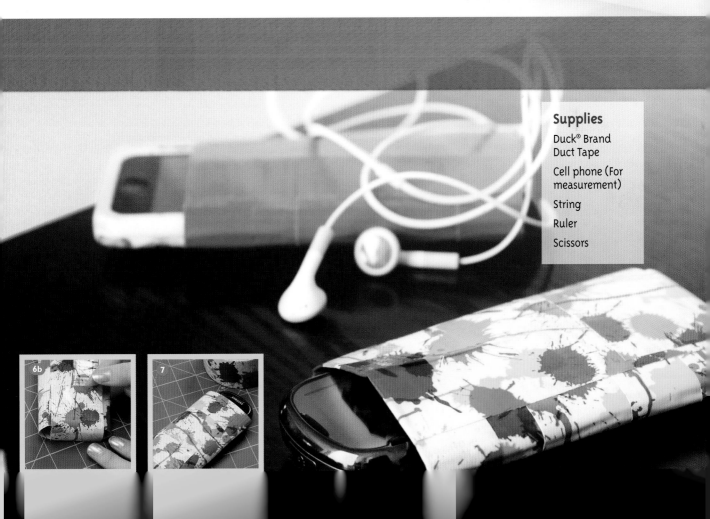

Daisy/ Daisy Pen

For multi colored flowers make the petals in 2 or 3 different colors of Duck® Tape Brand Duct Tape!

To make the stem:

1 Cut a piece of Duck® Tape that is long enough to cover the pen length-wise.

2 Place the pen on the outside edge of the Duck® Tape and roll the pen across to cover.

To make the flower center:

3 Cut a 6 inch piece of Duck® Tape to create the center of the flower and then cut the piece of tape in half length wise.

4 Cut the two strips of Duck® Tape into squares. (the same method used for making the rose petals for the Duck® Tape rose)

5 Sticky side up, fold one edge over itself, leaving some stickiness on the side and bottom.

6 Take the opposite edge and fold it over, leaving only stickiness on the bottom of the strip.

7 Take that piece of Duck® Tape and roll it around the top edge of the pen creating the center of the flower.

8 Repeat steps 5-7 to create the center of your flower. **Note:** You will need to make about 22-30 squares to create the center of the flower.

To make the flower petals:

9 Cut two pieces of Duck® Tape approximately 10 inches long and place it sticky side down on your flat surface.

10 Cut both pieces of tape in half and then cut the pieces of tape vertically so you have a total of 8 skinny tape strips.

11 Use wire cutters, cut a 3 inch piece of floral wire and place the wire toward the end of one of your tape strips.

12 Fold the top of the tape over, leaving the bottom half of the petal with the sticky side of the tape exposed.

13 Cut the folded side of the tape strip into a flower petal shape.

14 Take the petal and place the side with the adhesive showing on the stem and wrap the edges around it.

15 Repeat steps 11-14 until you have a total of 8 petals.

16 Cut a 2 inch piece of Duck® Tape and cut 4 squares out of it. Place each of the squares on opposite sides of each other at the base of the flower to create the petals for a smooth clean finish.

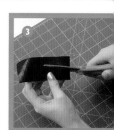

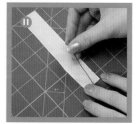

Supplies

Duck® Brand Duct Tape

Scissors

Craft Board

Bubble Wrap® brand cushioning

① Cut a piece of Bubble Wrap® that measures approximately 9 inches long by 4 inches wide and cover the edges with Duck® Tape, then cover the body with a piece of tape placed horizontally on the Bubble Wrap®.

② Create a cylinder shape by applying a strip of tape vertically where the edges meet. Make sure the strip covers the seam on the top, bottom, and inside of the cylinder.

③ To create the bottom of the koozie. Cut two strips of Duck® Tape —one measuring approximately 8 inches long and the second measuring 2 ½ inches long. Place the 2 ½ inch piece in the center of the 8 inch piece, sticky-side to sticky-side. Apply the exposed sticky ends of the strip to the bottom-sides of the koozie, making sure that it is not too tight or loose across the bottom.

④ Personalize your drink koozie to show your style, team spirit, and more!

Look for your favorite team's college logo design in College Duck® Tape.

Flip-Flops

1. Trace your foot or a pair of flip-flops on cardboard to figure out what size shoe you will need.

2. Use your scissors to cut out the traced design on the cardboard.

3. Take your desired color of Duck® Tape and cover the flip-flop horizontally starting at the top of the flip-flop. The seams of the tape should be on the bottom to insure clean lines on the top of the flip-flop.

4. Pick a different color of Duck® Tape to make the flip-flop strap.

5. Cut a 14 inch piece of Duck® Tape and lay it flat on the table. Fold in the sides, like a tri-fold, to make a long flat strip of tape.

6. Cut a hole in the top of your flip-flop, where your toe would be, and thread the tape through the hole.
Tape the middle of the strap to the bottom of the flip-flop.

7. Place the flip-flop on your foot to measure for the length of the loops. Once measured, tape the strap ends to the bottom of the shoe.

8. To keep the straps together in the center cut a 2 inch long piece of Duck® Tape, cut it in half, and wrap it around the middle of the straps to connect them together.

9. Cover the entire bottom of the flip-flop with a layer of Duck® Tape and cut the edges to create a clean edge.

10. Repeat all steps for the other foot.

Supplies

Duck® Brand Duct Tape

Cardboard

Pen

Scissors

Plastic flip-flops (optional)

Personalize your Duck® Tape flip-flops by adding your name or initials on the bottom of each shoe!

Hair Bow

① Make a double-sided Duck® Tape strip that is approximately 11 inches long by cutting two strips of Duck® Tape and sticking them sticky side to sticky side. This will create a sheet for your hair bow.

② Decorate your Duck® Tape fabric with stripes, polka dots or any creative design you can think of. For polka dots, use a pen to trace a coin on a strip of Duck® Tape and then cut out the circles. For stripes, cut long strips of various widths and colors and lay them on your Duck® Tape strip, then trim off the excess tape.

③ Fold your piece of Duck® Tape in half lengthwise (creating a crease), reopen it, and then bring both edges of the strip to the crease in the middle. Where the ends of the strip meet, pinch it together with your fingers. Cut a two- to three-inch strip of Duck® Tape, then cut it in half lengthwise and wrap it around the middle.

Attach the Duck® Tape hair bow to a hair clip or hair rubber band to accessorize any outfit.

Supplies
Duck® Brand Duct Tape
Ruler
Craft Board
Scissors
Pen (Optional)
Coin to use as a stencil for polka dots (Optional)

For an easy way to make polka dots and stripes for your hair bow use Duck® Tape Sheets with a grid lined backing.

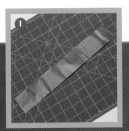

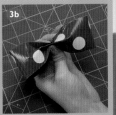

Luggage Tag

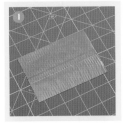

① Cut four pieces of Duck® Tape about 4 inches long. Lay two of the pieces of tape on your flat surface sticky side up. Make sure to overlap the edges slightly. Then place the other two pieces of tape on top of the first two pieces sticky side to sticky side. This will create a sheet of Duck® Tape.

② Using a permanent marker, write your name, address and phone number on your luggage tag.

③ Cut a small slit or punch a hole on one end of your luggage tag.

④ Feed a piece of yarn or a folded-over strip of Duck® Tape through and attach to your luggage. To make a folded-over Duck® Tape strip, cut a piece of Duck® Tape to your desired length. Fold it in half lengthwise and trim to your desired width.

⑤ Make your luggage tag out of brightly colored Duck® Tape and add stickers or fun designs to help your bag stand out when traveling!

Supplies
Duck® Brand Duct Tape
Scissors
Hole Punch
Yarn (Optional)
Stickers (Optional)
Permanent/Paint Markers (Optional)

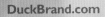

Supplies

Duck® Brand
Duck Tape

Scissors

Ruler

Picture to frame

Optional: stickers, string, decorative buttons and magnet strips

❶ Cut two 3¾ inch long pieces of Duck Tape and lay them both sticky side up on your work surface.

❷ Take one of the strips of tape and place it sticky side down on top of the other piece of tape creating a Duck Tape strip.

❸ Make two double-sided strips that are each 9½ inches long the same way you did the shorter strips in steps 1 & 2.

❹ Form the picture frame with the strips by placing the short pieces in between the long side pieces.

❺ Cut four 1 inch long strips. Use them to tape the frame together where the long and short pieces meet.

Note: These strips are place holders to hold the frame together.

❻ Cut two strips of Duck Tape, each 9 inches long. Place one of the 9 inch strips directly over one of the shorter sides of the frame, covering the place holders. Fold the extra tape onto the back.

❼ Repeat Step 6 on the opposite short side.

❽ Flip the picture frame over. Center the picture face down over the frame's window.

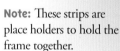

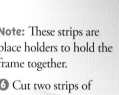

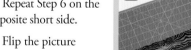
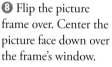
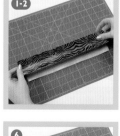

GO TEAM!

Cut two 9-inch strips. Use them to tape the picture onto the frame on the long sides.

Add magnetic strips to make a refrigerator or locker magnet.

Decorate with stickers, buttons or markers.

Attach a string to the back for a hanging picture.

Make a standing picture frame by taping a piece of cardboard onto the back.

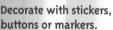

To create the body of the purse:

❶ Make a Duck® Tape fabric sheet that measures approximately 14 inches long by 5 strips wide.

❷ Trim excess tape to create a rectangle.

❸ To create the body of the purse fold the sheet in half, and tape the sides to seal the edges. Trim any excess.

To create the purse handle:

❹ Cut one strip of Duck® Tape slightly longer than the desired length for the purse strap and place it on your flat surface sticky side up.

❺ Cut another strip of Duck® Tape the same length and place it sticky side down on top of the first piece of tape. Make sure to leave about half of the sticky side of the tape exposed on each piece.

❻ Fold over the exposed sticky sides of tape creating a sturdy strap for your purse.

❼ Attach the strap to the purse with two 2 inch pieces of Duck® Tape securing the strap to the inside of the purse.

❽ Decorate your purse—use different colors and prints of Duck® Tape, jewels, and other embellishments!

Supplies

Duck® Brand Duct Tape

Craft Board

Scissors

Rose

Supplies

Duck® Brand Duct Tape

Straw

Scissors

1 Take your straw and cover it in Duck® Tape (lengthwise works the best). This step is completed best if you roll the straw across the tape, sticky-side up.

2 Cut several strips of Duck® Tape—approximately 2 inches each.

3 Sticky side up, fold one edge over itself, leaving some stickiness on the side and bottom.

4 Take the parallel edge and fold it over, leaving only stickiness on the bottom of the strip.

5 Roll this across tightly; this is your center.

6 Insert the center piece from Step 5 into the top of your straw.

7 Repeating Steps 2-4 with strips of Duck® Tape, loosely bind the strips around the center (these are your petals). Make sure to adhere the petals to both the straw and the center piece from Step 4. Continue until you've reached the desired size.

8 For the leaves under the rose, repeat Steps 2-4 with the same color that you used for the stem. Wrap these pieces around the stem at the base of the flower to cover up the tape edge.

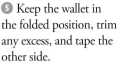

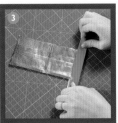

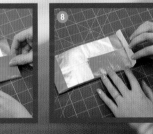
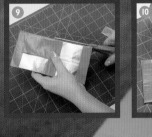

❶ Make a Duck® Tape fabric sheet that is 7 inches long by four strips wide.

❷ Fold the sheet in half so you have a rectangle.

❸ Use a piece of tape, about 4 inches long, to seal the edge on one of the short sides of the rectangle. Trim off the extra tape.

❹ Fold the wallet in half so the short sides line up. **Note:** Do this before taping the other side so that the wallet will fold without bulges.

❺ Keep the wallet in the folded position, trim any excess, and tape the other side.

❻ To make the pockets cut two 4 inch pieces of Duck® Tape and stick them together, sticky side to sticky side, making a Duck® Tape sheet. **Note:** Make sure to leave about ¼ inch of the sticky side of the tape exposed so it can stick to the wallet.

❼ Trim off the excess tape on the sides and stick the sheet in your wallet.

Duck® Tape Sheets (8.25 x 10 inches) are a quick and easy way to create a wallet in minutes!

❽ Cut one piece of Duck® Tape the same size as the piece that you used to seal the edges of the wallet. Place that piece of Duck® Tape over the edge of the packet and wrap it around the wallet just like in Step 3 to seal the edges. **Note:** Slit the sides of the credit card pockets where the tape seals the edges to fit credit cards in the slots.

❾ Repeat Steps 6-8 to add more pockets.

❿ Decorate the outside of your wallet with different shapes or designs and make it unique!

Supplies

Duck® Brand Duct Tape

Scissors

Ruler

Stickers, Permanent or Paint Markers (Optional)

Duck® Tape Sheets (Optional)

15

Wristlet

To create the wristlet body:

1 Create a sheet of Duck® Tape fabric that is approximately 10 inches long by 5 strips wide.

2 Once the sticky side of the sheet is covered, trim off any excess tape to make a rectangle.

3 To create the body of the wristlet fold the sheet in half and then tape the sides with Duck® Tape to seal the edges. Trim any excess.

Duck® Brand Duct Tape

Scissors

Craft Board

 To easily cut through Duck® Tape try titanium bonded scissors from Westcott® Brand.

To create the wristlet handle:

4 Cut one strip of tape slightly longer than the desired length of the purse handle (about 10 inches), and place it on your flat surface sticky side up.

5 Cut another strip of tape the same length and place it sticky side down on top of the first strip. Make sure to leave about half of the sticky side exposed on each piece.

6 Fold over the exposed sticky sides of tape creating a sturdy strap for your wristlet.

7 Attach the strap to the wristlet with two 2 inch pieces of Duck® Tape, securing the strap inside the wristlet.

8 Decorate your wristlet with different colors and prints of Duck® Tape, jewels, or other embellishments!

16

Westcott® is a registered trademark of Acme United Corporation.